MOST WANTED

DEADLIEST OCEAN CREATURES

John Perritano

SCHOLASTIC INC.

ISBN 978-1-338-67269-5

10 9 8   23 24

Printed in the U.S.A.   40
First printing 2020

Book produced by 22 MEDIAWORKS, INC.
lary@22MediaWorks.com
President LARY ROSENBLATT
Design and Production FABIA WARGIN DESIGN
Writer JOHN PERRITANO
Editor SUSAN ELKIN
Copy Editor LAURIE LIEB
Photo Researcher DAVID PAUL PRODUCTIONS

Photos ©: cover center: Pieter De Pauw/Getty Images; back cover: Bence Sibalin/Dreamstime; 4–5: lindsay_imagery/Getty Images; 8 top: Melanie Stetson Freeman/Getty Images; 9: National Geographic Image Collection/Alamy Stock Photo; 10: Joe Belanger/Alamy Stock Photo; 11 bottom: Magnus Larsson/Getty Images; 12 top left: blickwinkel/Alamy Stock Photo; 14: Tatiana Belova/Dreamstime; 15 top: Mietitore/Dreamstime; 16: Smitty Smitty/Dreamstime; 17: imageBROKER/Alamy Stock Photo; 18: Stocktrek Images, Inc./Alamy Stock Photo; 19: De Agostini Picture Library/Getty Images; 20 top: David Fleetham/Alamy Stock Photo; 20 bottom: Nature Picture Library/Alamy Stock Photo; 21: WaterFrame/Alamy Stock Photo; 22: Paulo Oliveira/Alamy Stock Photo; 24 top: Dwiputra18/Dreamstime; 26: Auscape International Pty Ltd/Alamy Stock Photo; 27: WaterFrame/Alamy Stock Photo; 30 bottom: Placebo365/Getty Images; 32: Mora0132/Dreamstime; blood splotches throughout: Eshmadeva/Dreamstime, Exe2be/Dreamstime, Zerbor/Dreamstime. All other photos © Shutterstock.com.

DEADLY DANGER IN THE SEA

The sea can look peaceful.
So quiet. So calm. A place of wonder.

BUT DEEP BELOW THE WAVES, DANGER LURKS.
There are monsters aplenty. Some are big. Many
are small. Some kill with **poison**. Many slash
other animals with razor-sharp teeth.

In this book, you will read about some of the
deadliest animals in the ocean. Some you may
have heard of, but others might be new to you.

Turn the page and read on if you dare...

*T*HE GREAT WHITE SHARK is one of the largest fish in the ocean. It can weigh as much as five thousand pounds and be as long as twenty feet.

Great whites are also the largest **predator** fish. That means they stalk other fish to eat. Sometimes great whites will swim in cool water by a shore. That can make them a danger to humans.

Great White Shark

Bull Shark

A great white has up to three hundred sharp teeth. One bite and a person can lose a leg or an arm.

Experts say that about one hundred shark attacks occur around the world each year. The great white shark is responsible for up to one-half of them. Most shark attacks are not deadly, though. That's because they don't really like human flesh. They would rather eat sea lions or seals.

Still, great white sharks are often blamed for attacking people. Many experts say that the bull shark, not the great white, is the most dangerous shark of all for humans.

DID YOU KNOW?

Great white sharks can smell blood and can tell if there's one drop in twenty-five gallons of water.

GREAT WHITE SHARK

Great White Shark

SCIENTIFIC NAME	Carcharodon carcharias	
TYPE Fish	DIET Carnivorous	
LENGTH 15 feet to more than 20 feet		
WEIGHT Up to 2.5 tons		

DEFINITION: CARNIVOROUS MEANS MEAT-EATING.

BARRACUDA

Great Barracuda

SCIENTIFIC NAME	Sphyraenidae	
TYPE Fish	**DIET** Carnivorous	
LENGTH 72 inches or more		

BARRACUDAS ARE SLEEK AND FAST. They can speed through the water at up to 35 miles per hour, so they can easily zero in on their **prey**.

The barracuda has two rows of sharp fangs in both its upper and lower jaws. Its bites can cause deep cuts.

Barracudas like to dine on large and small fish. They strike quickly, and they can swallow a big fish in one gulp. If they want to chow down on an even larger fish, they can rip it to shreds in one bite.

Barracudas don't usually attack humans, but sometimes they do. One man needed 255 stitches to repair a monstrous bite on his arm.

Diver and a large school of barracudas

DID YOU KNOW?

Barracudas carry poison in their flesh. If you ate barracuda meat, you might get food poisoning.

MOST PEOPLE THINK that jellyfish are more annoying than dangerous. Sure, their stings itch and hurt. But a jellyfish can't kill a person. Right?

Wrong!

One type of jellyfish is more dangerous than any shark. It's called the box jellyfish. Its deadly venom is usually passed through a bite or a sting.

Scientists say that the Australian box jellyfish is the most poisonous marine animal on the planet. If one of its ten-foot-long **tentacles** touches a swimmer or diver, that person may die from shock or heart failure before reaching the shore.

Another type of "boxie" won't kill a human. But when it does sting people, they might wish they were dead. The poison causes vomiting, agonizing headaches, and severe stomach pain.

DID YOU KNOW?

A box jellyfish can have up to 15 tentacles, each with about 5,000 stinging cells.

Box jellyfish lesions on a person's leg

Box Jellyfish

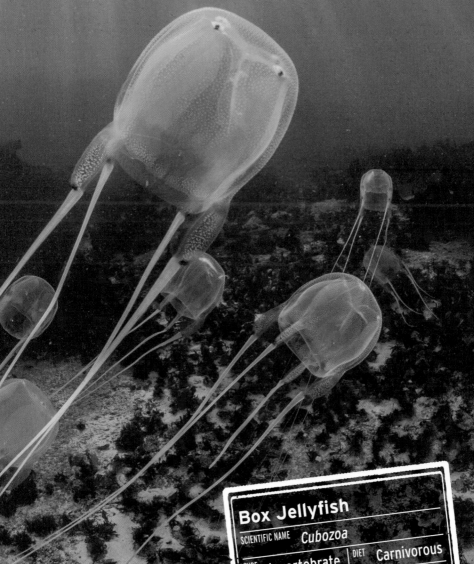

Box Jellyfish

SCIENTIFIC NAME	*Cubozoa*		
TYPE	Invertebrate	DIET	Carnivorous
LENGTH	10 feet long; 10 inches across		
WEIGHT	Up to 4.5 pounds		

Sea ANEMONE

Sea Anemone

SCIENTIFIC NAME Actiniaria

TYPE Invertebrate | DIET Carnivorous

DIAMETER 0.5 to 72 inches

THE YELLOW SEA ANEMONE can be mistaken for a beautiful underwater flower. But don't get too close. It's a poisonous animal.

Yellow Sea Anemone

Anemones spend most of their time attached to rocks and coral, where they wait for a fish to wander by. If the fish passes close enough, the anemone will stretch its venomous tentacles and shoot a harpoon-like thread, or dart, at the intruder.

That thread is filled with a toxin that can **paralyze** the fish. The anemone then uses its tentacles to guide the helpless creature into its mouth.

Gulp!

DID YOU KNOW?
Sea anemones are sticky to help them catch their food, as prey will stick to them.

Clownfish in a Magnificent Sea Anemone

Some fish can escape this fate, however. The colorful clownfish is one. Its body has a special coating of **mucus**, a type of slime, that protects it against the anemone's sting. Clownfish make their home in the anemone's tentacles. There, they are safe from predators.

11

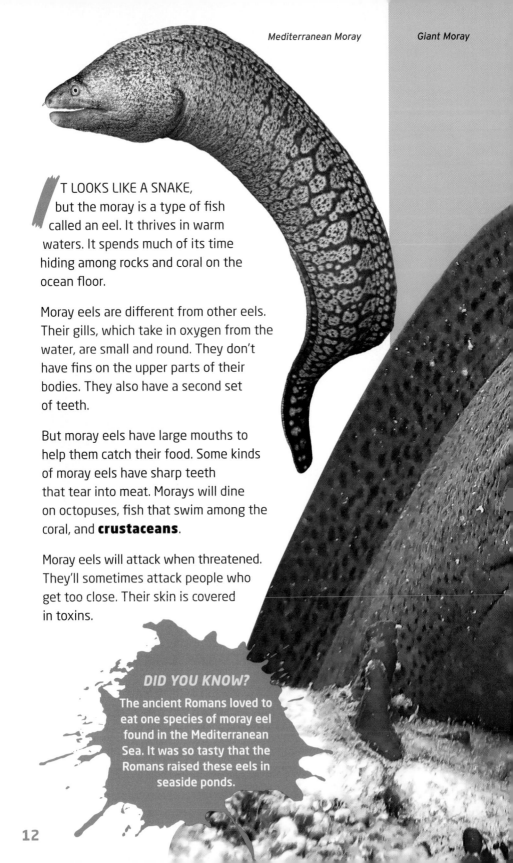

IT LOOKS LIKE A SNAKE, but the moray is a type of fish called an eel. It thrives in warm waters. It spends much of its time hiding among rocks and coral on the ocean floor.

Moray eels are different from other eels. Their gills, which take in oxygen from the water, are small and round. They don't have fins on the upper parts of their bodies. They also have a second set of teeth.

But moray eels have large mouths to help them catch their food. Some kinds of moray eels have sharp teeth that tear into meat. Morays will dine on octopuses, fish that swim among the coral, and **crustaceans**.

Moray eels will attack when threatened. They'll sometimes attack people who get too close. Their skin is covered in toxins.

DID YOU KNOW?

The ancient Romans loved to eat one species of moray eel found in the Mediterranean Sea. It was so tasty that the Romans raised these eels in seaside ponds.

Moray Eel

Moray Eel

SCIENTIFIC NAME	*Muraena helena*		
TYPE	Fish	DIET	Carnivorous
LENGTH	4 to 156 inches long		

PIRANHA

Piranha

N 2016, officials in Brazil told swimmers to stay out of the water. Why the warning? Because piranhas had attacked swimmers, injuring more than fifty people in one month.

Tourists were bitten on their hands and feet. One fish attacked the heel of a four-year-old boy.

Although piranhas never grow larger than two feet long, most people fear them. The fish live in the rivers and lakes of Central and South America. The Amazon River is home to up to twenty different species.

OW?

anhas
varn
vay.

Piranhas travel together in groups called shoals to protect themselves. They'll feed together in a frenzy, as if they've never eaten before.

The red-bellied piranha is one of the most dangerous of the species. It can eat a fish that is about one-eighth of its size.

THE STRIPED SURGEONFISH is one of the most beautiful creatures in the ocean. Its bright, rich colors make it look like a floating neon sign. People often keep these fish in aquariums.

Please do not touch one, though. It will cut you. Surgeonfish have spines along the base of their tails and on each side of their bodies. These spines are as sharp as a surgeon's scalpel, or knife. In fact, that's where the fish gets its name.

Not only are its spines sharp, but some surgeonfish species are also venomous. The venom can make humans sick, but it is rarely deadly. Although striped surgeonfish can be hazardous, they mostly like to eat **algae**. They also like to snack on tiny shellfish.

Striped surgeonfish live in the Indian and Pacific Oceans.

DID YOU KNOW?

They secrete mucus, slime, from their skin which provides protect against parasites and infections.

STRIPED SURGEONFISH

spine

Striped Surgeonfish

SCIENTIFIC NAME *Acanthurus lineatus*

TYPE **Fish**   DIET **Omnivorous**

LENGTH **10 to 15 inches**

DEFINITION: OMNIVOROUS MEANS PLANT- AND MEAT-EATING.

Oyster
Toadfish

Oyster Toadfish

SCIENTIFIC NAME *Opsanus tau*

TYPE Fish   DIET Omnivorous

LENGTH Up to 12 inches

WITH ITS OVERSIZED HEAD and frowny mouth, the oyster toadfish isn't the prettiest sea creature. This fish lives among oyster beds in the Chesapeake Bay, which borders Maryland and Virginia. Toadfish also hide in boat wrecks, among rocks, and in other concealed places.

Fishing crews do not like to catch oyster toadfish. These fish will flex the sharp spines on their dorsal fins and gills. They will snap and bite with powerful jaws. Many people have described its bite as feeling like being hit with a hammer.

The toadfish is a bottom feeder. That means that it eats whatever lies on the bottom of the bay. Its bite is so strong that it can crush the shells of **mollusks** and rip apart oysters, crabs, shrimps, squid, and other similar creatures.

DID YOU KNOW?

From April to October, it's not uncommon to hear the underwater foghorn call of male toadfish.

THE INDONESIAN NEEDLEFISH is not aggressive, venomous, or poisonous. Even its bites aren't that painful. But don't get in its way.

The needlefish, which is shaped like a narrow knife, swims mostly near the surface of the water. It can fly out of the water like a missile, reaching speeds of up to 37 miles per hour.

Because its jaws are so sharp and so long (up to three feet), the fish can turn itself into a flying spear. It will leap over the deck of a boat rather than swim around it. At night, needlefish are attracted to boat lights and the flashlights of divers.

DID YOU KN

One species needlefish li to swim alon tuna.

If a needlefish stabs you, the result isn't pretty. Its beak is so sharp that it can puncture your body.

INDONESIAN NEEDLEFISH

Indonesian Needlefish		
SCIENTIFIC NAME	*Tylosurus crocodilus*	
TYPE Fish	DIET	Carnivorous
LENGTH 20 inches		

Textile Cone Snail

Textile Cone Snail

SCIENTIFIC NAME	Conus textile
TYPE	Mollusk
DIET	Carnivorous
LENGTH	Average 4 to 6 inches

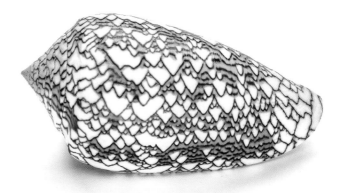

IF YOU'VE EVER SEEN A SLUG OR A SNAIL, chances are you didn't run away scared. But if you ever come across a textile cone snail, get away as fast as you can.

A cone snail doesn't look frightening, but it can fire a poisonous "harpoon" at its prey. One touch and the toxin paralyzes the animal. One stab in the ankle from a cone snail can kill a person.

Scientists have discovered about five hundred species of cone snails. Some will target sleeping fish or worms. Some cone snails will eat other mollusks. The snails tend to hunt when it's dark. They have a good sense of smell that will lead them to their prey.

When a textile cone snail finds something it wants to eat, it will extend a tube-like structure called a proboscis.

DID YOU KNOW?

The textile cone snail's venom has been used to create a medicine to treat chronic pain.

Fire One! The snail releases its harpoon—a poisonous tooth. Once the harpoon strikes the prey, the snail will drag the "hooked" prey into its mouth.

Anything the textile cone snail can't digest, including its harpoon, it will spit out.

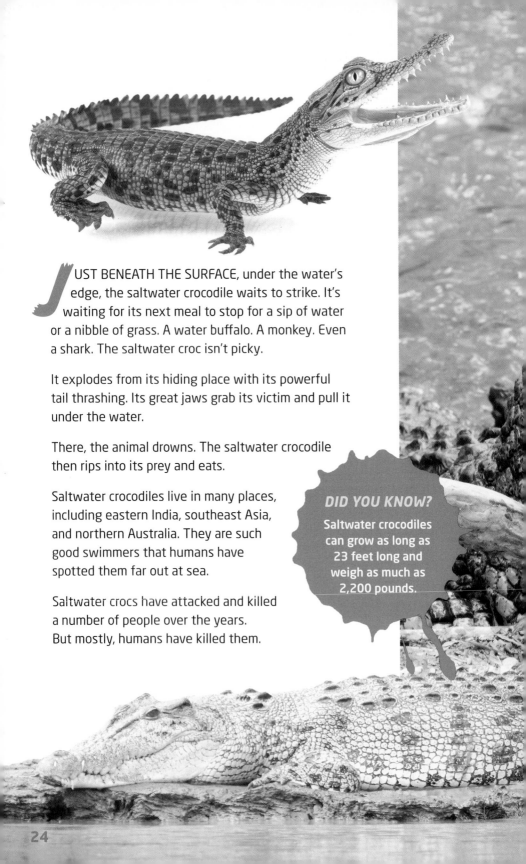

JUST BENEATH THE SURFACE, under the water's edge, the saltwater crocodile waits to strike. It's waiting for its next meal to stop for a sip of water or a nibble of grass. A water buffalo. A monkey. Even a shark. The saltwater croc isn't picky.

It explodes from its hiding place with its powerful tail thrashing. Its great jaws grab its victim and pull it under the water.

There, the animal drowns. The saltwater crocodile then rips into its prey and eats.

Saltwater crocodiles live in many places, including eastern India, southeast Asia, and northern Australia. They are such good swimmers that humans have spotted them far out at sea.

Saltwater crocs have attacked and killed a number of people over the years. But mostly, humans have killed them.

DID YOU KNOW?

Saltwater crocodiles can grow as long as 23 feet long and weigh as much as 2,200 pounds.

SALTWATER CROCODILE

Saltwater Crocodile

SCIENTIFIC NAME **Crocodylus porosus**

TYPE **Reptile**   DIET **Carnivorous**

LENGTH **Average 17 feet long**

BLUE-RINGED OCTOPUS

Blue-Ringed Octopus

SCIENTIFIC NAME
Hapalochlaena maculosa
and *Hapalochlaena lunulata*

TYPE	Mollusk	DIET	Carnivorous

LENGTH
Up to 4 inches including tentacles

Hapalochlaena maculosa

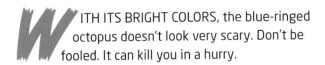

WITH ITS BRIGHT COLORS, the blue-ringed octopus doesn't look very scary. Don't be fooled. It can kill you in a hurry.

Although this octopus is only the size of a golf ball, it is dangerous. It packs enough venom to kill twenty-six humans in mere minutes. Scientists say it is one of the deadliest creatures in the ocean.

The venom is produced by bacteria inside the animal's saliva glands. The poison is more powerful than any poison produced by any animal on land. The blue-ringed octopus uses its venom to hunt.

When it catches a crab or small fish, the octopus pecks at its prey with its beak, opening a small hole. The octopus then injects its venom to kill its prey.

J KNOW?

a blue-ringed
n't cause pain
ut by the time
es out they've
may be too late
n from death.

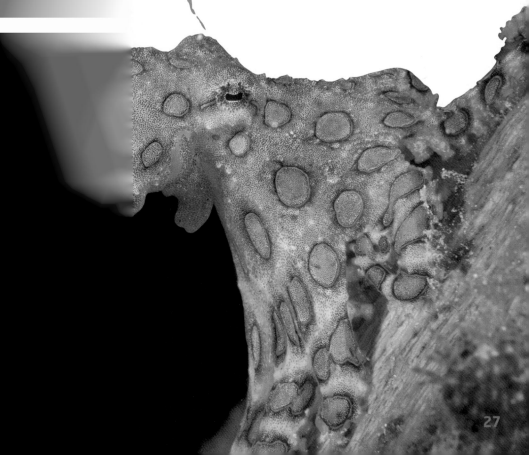

WHEN PREDATORS THREATEN A PUFFERFISH, this strange-looking creature puffs up like a balloon. It fills its stretchy stomach with water or air to scare off anything that comes too close.

If a predator grabs hold of a pufferfish before it inflates, the fish will leave more than a bad taste in the predator's mouth. Most pufferfish contain poison that tastes awful. It can also kill. In fact, there's enough poison in one pufferfish to kill thirty human adults.

Some puffers also have sharp spines on their skin, which they use to defend themselves.

Although pufferfish are highly toxic, some Japanese diners consider it a treat. A pufferfish meal is called *fugu*. Only a trained chef can prepare the fish for a meal. If the chef doesn't prepare the fish correctly, it means certain death for a diner.

DID YOU KNOW?

Pufferfish are also known as blowfish.

Valentin's Sharpnose Pufferfish

Yellow Blackspotte Pufferfish

PUFFERFISH

Pufferfish

SCIENTIFIC NAME: *Tetraodontidae*

TYPE: Fish

DIET: Carnivorous

LENGTH: Up to 3 feet

More Deadly Creatures

Here are more of the world's Most Wanted sea creatures

LIONFISH

Found mostly in the Pacific and Indian Oceans, lionfish are among the most beautiful creatures in the sea. Many have white, brown, or maroon stripes. Their fins look like a fan. But the spines of a lionfish can deliver a toxin by creating a hole in its prey.

STONEFISH

The stonefish is among the most venomous fish in the sea. It can grow up to fifteen inches long. To capture its meal, a stonefish waits for its prey to swim by. Then it will attack quickly. It uses venom to protect itself. It won't attack humans, but if you step on one, get to a doctor fast. If the injury is left untreated, the pain will be unbearable. In some cases, a person might die.

SEA SNAKE

Sea snakes look like snakes because—well, that's what they are. Sea snakes are venomous. The deadliest is the beaked sea snake. One drop of its venom is enough to kill about three humans. It will also defend itself by spraying a sticky liquid, much like a skunk does.

FLOWER URCHIN

The flower urchin is no flower. Although beautiful, flower urchins are highly venomous sea animals without a backbone. They are related to starfish and sea cucumbers. They are the deadliest urchins in the ocean. Their "flowers" are tiny claws. Touch one and you will experience severe pain. You might have difficulty breathing. Your lips and eyelids will become numb.

Green Moray Eel

GLOSSARY

algae small plants without roots or stems that grow in or near water

crustacean a sea creature that has an outer skeleton and several pairs of legs, such as a crab or lobster

mollusk an animal with no spine and a soft body, usually protected by a hard outer shell, like clams and oysters

mucus a slimy material that forms a protective coating for animals

paralyze to make a person or animal unable to move or function

poison a substance that can harm another living creature if it is touched or swallowed

predator an animal that survives by hunting other animals for food

prey an animal that is hunted by another animal for food

tentacles the long, flexible limbs of an animal, such as the octopus or squid